D0894010

CHARLES B. & PATRICIA A.

TUBBS
CHILDREN'S
LIBRARY

Ducks on the Farm

by Mari C. Schuh

Consulting Editor: Gail Saunders-Smith, Ph.D.

Consultant: Cary J. Trexler, Ph.D., Assistant Professor
California Agricultural Experiment Station
University of California, Davis

Pebble Books

an imprint of Capstone Press
Mankato, Minnesota

Pebble Books are published by Capstone Press
151 Good Counsel Drive, P.O. Box 669, Mankato, Minnesota 56002
http://www.capstone-press.com

1 2 3 4 5 6 08 07 06 05 04 03

Library of Congress Cataloging-in-Publication Data
Schuh, Mari C., 1975–
    Ducks on the farm / by Mari C. Schuh.
    p. cm.—(On the farm)
    Summary: Photographs and simple text describe ducks and the lives they live
on the farm.
    Includes bibliographical references and index.
    ISBN 0-7368-1661-5 (hardcover)
    1. Ducks—Juvenile literature. [1. Ducks.] I. Title. II.. Series: Schuh, Mari C.,
1975– . On the farm.
SF505.3.S38 2003
636.5'97—dc21   2002009477

Note to Parents and Teachers

The On the Farm series supports national science standards related
to life science. This book describes and illustrates domestic ducks
and their lives on the farm. The photographs support early readers
in understanding the text. The repetition of words and phrases
helps early readers learn new words. This book also introduces
early readers to subject-specific vocabulary words, which are
defined in the Words to Know section. Early readers may need
assistance to read some words and to use the Table of Contents,
Words to Know, Read More, Internet Sites, and Index/Word List
sections of the book.

Table of Contents

Ducks are birds.

Some ducks are wild.

Some ducks live on farms.

Some ducks live on small farms. They often live near water. Other ducks live on large farms.

A male is a drake. A female is a duck. Young ducks are ducklings.

Farmers raise ducks
for their eggs, meat,
and feathers.

Some farmers raise
ducks for hunting.
Other farmers use ducks
to train sheep dogs.

Farmers feed corn and soybean meal to ducks.

Ducks have webbed feet. They waddle when they walk.

Ducks have waterproof feathers. Ducks preen.

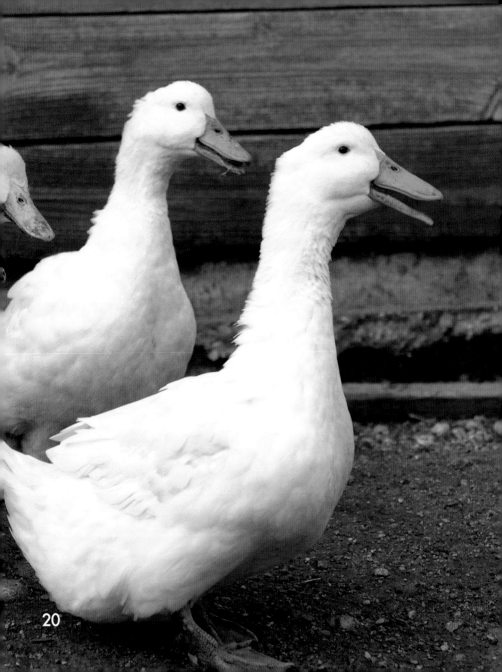

Ducks quack.

Words to Know

feather—one of the light, fluffy parts that covers a bird's body; duck feathers often are used in pillows, jackets, and sleeping bags.

hunting—shooting and killing animals for food or sport

preen—to clean and arrange feathers with a beak; ducks spread oil from their body on their feathers when they preen; this keeps their feathers waterproof.

sheep dog—a farm dog that herds groups of sheep; dogs sometimes herd ducks to learn how to herd sheep and other animals.

soybean—a seed that grows in pods on a bushy plant; farmers feed ducks a corn and soybean meal mixture that has vitamins and minerals.

waddle—to walk with short steps while moving from side to side

webbed—having folded skin or tissue between an animal's toes or fingers; webbed feet help ducks swim better.

Read More

Gibbons, Gail. *Ducks!* New York: Holiday House, 2001.

Mitchell, Melanie. *Ducks.* First Step Nonfiction. Minneapolis: Lerner, 2003.

Watts, Barrie. *Duck.* Watch It Grow. Mankato, Minn.: Smart Apple Media, 2002.

Internet Sites

Track down many sites about ducks.
Visit the FACT HOUND at *http://www.facthound.com*

IT IS EASY! IT IS FUN!

1) Go to *http://www.facthound.com*

2) Type in: 0736816615

3) Click on "FETCH IT" and FACT HOUND will find several links hand-picked by our editors.

Relax and let our pal FACT HOUND do the research for you!

Index/Word List

birds, 5
corn, 15
drake, 9
ducklings, 9
eggs, 11
farmers, 11,
  13, 15
farms, 5, 7
feathers,
  11, 19
feed, 15
feet, 17
female, 9

hunting, 13
large, 7
live, 5, 7
male, 9
meat, 11
other, 7, 13
preen, 19
quack, 21
raise, 11, 13
sheep dogs,
  13
small, 7
some, 5, 7, 13

soybean meal,
  15
train, 13
use, 13
waddle, 17
walk, 17
water, 7
waterproof,
  19
webbed, 17
wild, 5
young, 9

Word Count: 91
Early-Intervention Level: 11

Credits
Heather Kindseth, series designer; Patrick D. Dentinger, book designer;
Deirdre Barton, photo researcher

Capstone Press/Gary Sundermeyer, cover, 1, 6 (top), 12, 14, 16, 18, 20
Metzer Farms/John Metzer, 6 (bottom), 8, 10
Visuals Unlimited/Adrian Corton, 4